D0743234

Dates of a Decade

# THE 1960s

## Nathaniel Harris

with additional text by Jacqueline Laks Gorman

ARCTURUS

This edition first published by Arcturus Publishing
Distributed by Black Rabbit Books
123 South Broad Street
Mankato
Minnesota MN 56001

Copyright © 2009 Arcturus Publishing Limited

Printed in the United States

Series concept: Alex Woolf
Editor and picture researcher: Alex Woolf
U.S. editor: Jacqueline Laks Gorman
Designer: Phipps Design

Library of Congress Cataloging-in-Publication Data

Harris, Nathaniel, 1937-
  The 1960s / Nathaniel Harris.
      p. cm. -- (Dates of a decade)
  Includes index.
  ISBN 978-1-84837-282-5 (hardcover)
  1.  History, Modern--1945-1989--Juvenile literature.  I. Title.
II. Title: Nineteen sixties.
  D842.5.H37 2010
  909.82'6--dc22

                                2009000006

Picture credits:
Corbis: 5 (Hulton-Deutsch Collection), 7 (Bettmann), 8 (Bettmann), 9, 10 (© The
Andy Warhol Foundation for the Visual Arts, Inc. / DACS, London, 2007. Trademarks
Licensed by Campbell Soup Company. All Rights Reserved.), 11 (© Bridget Riley,
all rights reserved / Hulton-Deutsch Collection), 12, 13 (Bettmann), 14 (Bettmann),
15 (Flip Schulke), cover (right) and 16 (Bettmann), 18 (Bettmann), 19 (Bettmann),
20 (Bettmann), 21 (Tim Page), 24 (Bettmann), 25 (Bettmann), 27 (Hulton-Deutsch
Collection), 28 (Bettmann), 30 (Hulton-Deutsch Collection), 31 (Burlot
Jacques/Sygma), 32 (Alain Nogues/Sygma), cover (bottom) and 33 (epa), cover
(top) and 35, 36 (Christine Spengler/Sygma), 37 (Michael Brennan), 39 (Henry
Diltz), 40 (E. Petersen/Bettmann), 41 (J.P. Laffont/Sygma), 42 (Frank
Wolfe/Bettmann), 45 (Bettmann).
Getty Images: 23 (Hulton Archive), 26 (Hulton Archive), 38 (Time & Life Pictures),
43 (Arnold Sachs/Hulton Archive), 44 (James Flores/NFL).
Rex Features: 17 (Everett Collection).
Science Photo Library: 34 (NASA).
Topham Picturepoint: 4.

# Contents

## GLOBAL EVENTS

## UNITED STATES EVENTS

# Massacre at Sharpeville

At about 1:40 in the afternoon, South African police fired machine guns, rifles, and revolvers into a crowd of several thousand men, women, and children. The crowd fled, but the police continued to fire. Of the 69 dead and 300 injured, many were shot in the back.

The massacre ended a standoff that had begun early that morning when black demonstrators surrounded the police station at Sharpeville. The station was protected by a wire fence, 200 heavily armed policemen and Saracen armored cars. During the morning, more and more people arrived. The police were reinforced and a few arrests were made without any resistance being offered. The only independent witnesses described the crowd as good-humored and not expecting trouble, although some children flung a few stones. It seems certain that nobody was armed. Unnerved by the size and movements of the crowd, the police opened fire, apparently without receiving orders to do so.

## Apartheid

The Sharpeville massacre had a great impact on world opinion. It confirmed the brutally racist nature of South Africa, a country run by and for the white minority. The black majority had no votes and were mostly very poor. In theory, South Africa was not racist but followed a

*Sharpeville: security forces move in after the massacre. For a long time the South African authorities tried to blame the victims, rather than their own forces, for what had happened.*

policy of apartheid: The different races would live and develop in separate communities, including "homelands" set aside for black Africans. But these homelands were all poor, overcrowded areas where it was hard to make a living. In practice, "all-white" towns and industries needed black labor, so black workers were assembled in "townships" like Sharpeville just outside them. Townships were large but primitively equipped settlements rather than true towns.

Black Africans who lived and worked outside the homelands had to carry a passbook – a kind of identity card – at all times. Passbooks restricted their movements and separated families. They became one of the most bitterly resented symbols of oppression, and the demonstration at Sharpeville was part of a nationwide protest against the pass laws.

## After Sharpeville

After the shooting, the South African government remained unyielding. All black political movements were outlawed and no concessions were made. Apartheid seemed immovable until the late 1980s, when it began to crumble. Finally, in 1990, the imprisoned black leader Nelson Mandela was released and South Africa set out on the road to democracy.

*For whites only: as the sign makes clear, this Cape Town beach is for public use, but only by whites. Such unfair discrimination was typical of South Africa's infamous system of apartheid (separation).*

## eye witness

The crowd seemed perfectly amiable…. Then the shooting started. We heard the chatter of a machine gun, then another, then another…. One woman was hit about ten yards from our car. Her companion, a young man, went back when she fell. He thought she had stumbled. Then he turned her over and saw that her chest had been shot away. He looked at the blood on his hand and said: "My God, she's gone!" Hundreds of kids were running, too.

Humphrey Tyler, assistant editor of the South African magazine *Drum*, writing in the March 21, 1960 issue

• **SEE ALSO**
Pages 6–7: June 30, 1960: The Congo Gains its Independence
Pages 14–15: August 28, 1963: The "I Have a Dream" Speech

• **FURTHER INFORMATION**
Books:
*Sharpeville* by Sarah Harris (Dryad, 1998)
Websites:
africanhistory.about.com/library/weekly/aa-SharpevilleMassacre-a.htm
A useful African history site

# The Congo Gains its Independence

For 80 years, the Congo, a vast area in central Africa, was a colony ruled by Belgium. The colonial rulers benefited greatly from the colony's mineral wealth, yet did little to educate or improve the lives of the overwhelming majority of black Congolese. Growing discontent alarmed the Belgians, who decided that it was time to leave. Hasty elections were held, and on June 30, 1960, Patrice Lumumba, the leader of the largest political party, became prime minister of the new state. The independence ceremony revealed how differently Belgians and black Africans viewed the colonial past (see sidebar).

## eye witness

It might have been guessed that the launching of the new Republic of Congo would prove a stormy affair…. The King declared, "For eighty years Belgium has sent your land the best of her sons…. It is your job, gentlemen, to show that we were right in trusting you." Lumumba … spoke many times of the "indispensable struggle to put an end to the humiliating slavery which was imposed on us by force…. Who will forget the rifle-fire from which so many of our brothers perished, or the jails in to which they were brutally thrown?"

The special correspondent of the *Guardian*, July 1, 1960

## Chaos and conflict

Such a rapid and unprepared handover was bound to cause trouble. Almost at once, fighting broke out between different Congolese groups. Europeans were attacked, and the army mutinied against its white officers. On July 11, the president of the copper-rich Katanga province, Moise Tshombe, announced that the province had broken away from the Congo. A very confused situation developed in which Congolese politicians vied for power while their forces tried to recover Katanga. Belgian and United Nations troops became involved, and great power rivalries even came into play when Lumumba secured help from the Soviet Union. However, Lumumba lost the struggle. He was imprisoned and then handed over to Katanga, where he was killed, supposedly trying to escape. Fighting went on until 1963, when Katanga admitted defeat. The unity of the Congo had been preserved, but General Sese Seko Mobutu, head of the Congolese army, emerged as the real power in the country. In 1965, Mobutu thrust the politicians aside, made himself president of Zaire (as the Congo was now called), and began a 32-year reign of tyranny and corruption.

*The doomed premier: Congo's first elected prime minister, Patrice Lumumba, under arrest, his arms tied behind him. Having lost a power struggle with the president, Lumumba was held by the troops of army chief Mobutu, beaten in front of television cameras, and handed over to his enemies in Katanga, where he was executed in January 1961.*

## Decolonization

The Congo was a chaotic example of decolonization – the end of rule by European states over most of Africa. Decolonization began in 1957, when Britain's Gold Coast colony became independent as Ghana, and continued all through the 1960s. By 1974, the colonial era was over. But in two former colonies, South Africa and Rhodesia (now Zimbabwe), the white minorities living in the country clung on to power for much longer. Africa remained a troubled continent. Most of the newly independent states either opted for single-party rule or experienced frequent military coups. In the 1970s, many of them slid into debt, with serious consequences, including poverty and instability, that were still holding them back in the 2000s.

- **SEE ALSO**
  Pages 4–5: March 21, 1960:
  Massacre at Sharpeville
  Pages 24–25: May 30, 1967:
  Biafra Breaks Away from Nigeria

- **FURTHER INFORMATION**
  Books:
  *Flashpoints: Central Africa* by Nicola Barber (Franklin Watts, 2005)
  Websites:
  www.bbc.co.uk/worldservice/africa/features/storyofafrica/14chapter7.shtml
  BBC's Story of Africa site

# 13 AUGUST 1961

# The Berlin Wall Rises

East German forces set to work early in the morning, long before it was light. By the time most citizens of Berlin were up, the East Germans had surrounded the western part of the city with barbed wire. Within a week the barbed wire had largely been replaced by a wall of concrete. Eventually, this Berlin Wall would become a still more formidable barrier, with watch towers manned by armed guards who shot at anyone who tried to cross into West Berlin without authorization. Over the next 28 years, hundreds would be killed attempting to escape from the East to the West.

## The Cold War

Berlin was on the front line in the Cold War being waged between the Western, U.S.-led alliance and the Eastern, Soviet-led bloc. It was "cold" because mutual hostility never turned into a "hot", shooting war between the major powers – although their growing nuclear arsenals caused worldwide alarm. In Europe, the most sensitive Cold War frontier ran between the pro-Western German Federal Republic (West Germany) and the German Democratic Republic (East Germany), which belonged in the Soviet camp.

Berlin's situation was exceptional. As a result of arrangements made between the victorious powers after World War II (1939–1945), West Berlin was part of the Federal Republic, though it lay deep inside East Germany.

*Building the Berlin Wall: a construction worker adds more large blocks to the steadily rising wall, designed to prevent discontented East German citizens from fleeing to West Berlin, part of the rival West German state.*

## What the papers said

The scream of sirens and the clank of steel on cobblestones echoed down the mean, dark streets. Frightened East Berliners peeked from behind their curtains to see military convoys stretching for blocks.... When dawn came ... a wall divided East Berlin from West Berlin.... The Wall was illegal, immoral and strangely revealing – illegal because it violated the Communists' solemn contracts to permit free movement throughout the city; immoral because it virtually jailed millions of innocent people; revealing because it advertised to all the world the failure of East Germany's Communist system.

*Time, August 25, 1961*

*John F. Kennedy views the wall from West Berlin, June 26, 1963. He is about to deliver a famous speech in praise of the hard-pressed Berliners.*

It became an outpost of the Western way of life, which was visibly freer and more prosperous than the communist system imposed by the Soviet Union on East Germany and other East European states. In spite of severe travel restrictions, East Germans fled to the West in huge numbers (2.5 million between 1949 and 1961), embarrassing the government and undermining the economy.

The easiest way to leave East Germany was by slipping through the city's streets, gardens, and canals into West Berlin. In July 1961, a time of East-West political tension, a staggering 30,000 East Germans left. The rapid erection of the Berlin Wall was the response – supposedly to keep out spies and radicals, but actually to keep the citizens in. The Western powers protested, and U.S. President John F. Kennedy made a famous speech declaring his solidarity with the beleaguered Berliners. But there was nothing to be done without risking war. The Berlin Wall stood until the 1989–1990 collapse of the communist system it was built to protect.

- **SEE ALSO**
  Pages 12–13: October 22, 1962:
  The Cuban Missile Crisis

  Pages 32–33: August 20, 1968:
  Soviet Forces Invade Czechoslovakia

- **FURTHER INFORMATION**
  📖 Books:
  *Days that Shook the World: The Fall of the Berlin Wall* by Pat Levy (Wayland, 2002)
  🖰 Websites:
  www.dw-world.de/dw/article/
  0,2144,2130235,00.html
  The construction of the Berlin Wall

# Soup Cans Sighted in Los Angeles

On July 9, 1962, the Ferns Gallery in Los Angeles staged the first one-man show by Andy Warhol, an artist who was still not well known. Each of the 32 paintings in the exhibition was a careful copy of a Campbell's soup can; the only difference between one picture and the next was the variety of soup named on the painted label. The show made an impact, impressing some spectators and puzzling or annoying others. When it moved to New York in the autumn, it became an undoubted success. Within a remarkably short time, Andy Warhol became the superstar of the movement known as Pop art.

## Pop art

Pop art was controversial and, some thought, not art at all. It drew heavily on well-known images from the mass media such as movies, TV, advertising and comic books. Its typical subjects were celebrities and models, cars, food, and other everyday branded consumer goods. It was bright, often gaudy, and usually cheerful. These qualities, along with the familiarity of its images, gave Pop art a wider public appeal than most art movements. It was excitingly modern-minded and consumer-conscious, reflecting the prosperity of the 1960s and the optimism and irreverence of a period when young people had more freedom and money to spend than ever before.

## Comic books and giant hamburgers

Some artists had been working in Pop-like styles from the mid-1950s, but 1962 was the year Pop art took off. Roy Lichtenstein's exhibition showed the works that made him, after Warhol, the most famous Pop artist – paintings of comic-book scenes, greatly enlarged but complete with the "balloons" that told readers what a character was saying or thinking. Lichtenstein even painted in the visible

*A Campbell's soup can, tomato variety: one of the repeated images that made Andy Warhol a famous Pop artist.*

dots that made up the original, crudely printed image. The Swedish-born sculptor Claes Oldenburg also came to the fore in 1962. He exhibited giant hamburgers and also achieved unusual effects with soft vinyl versions of objects such as typewriters.

Many Pop artists not only admired mass-media images but copied the mechanical methods used to reproduce them. Warhol used a technique known as screen-printing to produce multiple images of celebrities such as the film star Marilyn Monroe, singer Elvis Presley, and Chinese leader Mao Zedong. Britain also produced many Pop artists, including Richard Hamilton, Peter Blake, and Allen Jones. The style dominated the 1960s, gradually giving way to new trends in the early 1970s.

*Leading British artist Bridget Riley stands in front of one of her works in the 1960s Op art style, of which she was a pioneer. Op stood for "optical," referring to the illusion of vibrating movement experienced by a viewer when looking at this kind of picture. Op art had a strong influence, not only on art but on 1960s fashions in clothes.*

# What the papers said

The paintings appear to be uncompromisingly faithful to detail. Mr. Warhol's painting *Turkey Vegetable*, for example, is the twin of his equally honest *Chicken Noodle*, except for the words "turkey vegetable" and "chicken noodle." The total effect, I thought, was one of seeing perhaps more paintings of soup cans than one might care to see. I suspected for a moment, even, that Mr. Warhol might have had his tongue in his cheek…. I took a final look at Warhol's *Consomme*. I noticed the first "m" was larger than the second…. Perhaps, I mused, Warhol had been trying to tell us something there.

Jack Smith in the *Los Angeles Times*, July 23, 1962

- **SEE ALSO**
Pages 18–19: February 8, 1964: Beatlemania Hits the United States
Pages 38–39: August 15, 1969: The First Day at Woodstock

- **FURTHER INFORMATION**
Books:
*Artists in Profile: Pop Artists* by Paul Mason (Heinemann, 2003)
Websites:
www.popartists.com
A gallery of pop artists

# 22 OCTOBER 1962

# The Cuban Missile Crisis

A frightening episode in the Cold War began on Monday October 22, 1962, when U.S. President John F. Kennedy made a broadcast to the American people. He told them that the United States was under threat from nearby Cuba. Soviet teams on the island were secretly constructing nuclear missile sites, and the missiles themselves were being brought to Cuba by Soviet vessels. Kennedy announced a U.S. "quarantine" – in effect, a blockade of Cuba. Any ships carrying armaments would be turned back by the U.S. Navy. As 25 Soviet vessels were heading for Cuba, it seemed likely that they would refuse to submit to a search. And if that led to an armed clash, it might trigger a nuclear war.

*The closest of allies: Cuban leader Fidel Castro and the Soviet Union's Khrushchev embrace after meeting for the first time in 1960 at the United Nations General Assembly.*

## Cuba under Castro

The origins of the crisis lay in the U.S.-Cuban hostility that developed after Fidel Castro and his followers took power on the island in January 1959. Having ousted a corrupt dictatorship, Castro introduced a number of reforms, some of which injured U.S. economic interests. A U.S.-backed attempt to overthrow Castro failed humiliatingly, and U.S. anger increased as Cuba became closely allied with its Cold War adversary, the Soviet Union.

To Americans, establishing nuclear bases on Cuba was an intolerable threat. From the Soviet point of view, protecting an endangered ally was legitimate, and nuclear sites on Cuba were no different from the U.S. bases established near the Soviet bloc, including those recently established on the Soviet frontier with Turkey.

## Khrushchev and Kennedy

However, both the Soviet leader, Nikita Khrushchev, and President Kennedy realized that the two sides had so many weapons that a nuclear war would wreck the planet and possibly destroy the human race. They wanted to avoid war, but without backing down. On October 24, some Cuba-bound ships turned back, while the United States allowed other vessels through without searching them. But work on the missile sites went on, and a U.S. invasion of Cuba seemed imminent.

Then, on the 27th and 28th, an exchange of messages led to an agreement. The Soviet sites would be dismantled in return for a U.S. promise not to attack Cuba. Secretly, Kennedy also promised to remove U.S. bases in Turkey. Since this was not known, Kennedy appeared to have stood firm and was hailed in the West as a hero. In fact, Kennedy and Khrushchev had together – against the wishes of some of their close advisers – saved the world from catastrophe.

*Exit strategy: the U.S. blockade of Cuba ended when the Soviets agreed to remove their missiles from the island. But U.S. ships continued to monitor the situation. Here, the USS Barry (front) steams alongside the Soviet freighter Ansov, which has left Cuba laden with military hardware.*

## What the papers said

Last night's grim speech [by President Kennedy] was a new turn in the Kennedy–Khrushchev relationship, a calculated risk and one full of danger. But the President saw no acceptable alternative because, as he said, "the greatest danger of all would be to do nothing".... Certainly in the nuclear war that the President spoke of last night as a possibility "even the fruits of a victory would be ashes in our mouths." But there are times in history when men and nations must act. The President has judged this as such a moment.

*The Washington Post, October 23, 1962*

- **FURTHER INFORMATION**
- Books:
  *History Through Newspapers: The Cuban Missile Crisis* by Nathaniel Harris (Wayland 2002)
- Websites:
  library.thinkquest.org/11046
  Fourteen Days in October: the Cuban Missile Crisis – an interactive site

# The "I Have a Dream" Speech

Over 200,000 marchers, black and white, assembled in the U.S. capital, Washington, D.C., to demand full civil rights for African Americans. One of the march's leaders, Martin Luther King, made a speech from the steps of the Lincoln Memorial that has never been forgotten. In the rhythmic tones of a preacher, he said, again and again, "I have a dream." The dream was one in which black and white would live together in equality and brotherhood, with all hatred and bitterness put aside. He ended with a vision of all humanity "free at last!"

## Slavery and segregation

Black people had often been treated badly in the United States. The ancestors of America's black population had come to the country as slaves, taken by force from their African homes. Concentrated in the South, they became free only when President Abraham Lincoln abolished slavery during the Civil War (1861–1865).

*Martin Luther King makes his famous "I have a dream" speech in front of the Lincoln Memorial in Washington, D.C., at the end of the Freedom March for racial equality.*

However, their freedom was limited in practice, because the southern states passed local laws designed to hold them down. It was made as difficult as possible for blacks to become registered voters, let alone hold public office. Whites had priority in jobs and housing, and a policy of segregation forced blacks to use separate and usually inferior schools, transportation facilities, and restaurants.

## Civil rights

Things began to change in December 1955 after a black woman named Rosa Parks refused to give up her seat in a bus to a white man in Montgomery, Alabama. Parks was fined, but the incident ignited a determined civil rights movement. As it gathered strength, a Baptist minister, Martin Luther King, emerged as its most effective leader. King preached, and practiced, nonviolent action, although he and his followers in the South faced arrests, beatings, and, in some instances, killings.

The August 1963 demonstration and King's speech impressed the world and led to the 1964 Civil Rights Act, which showed a new resolve to end segregation and other injustices. King remained in the forefront of the movement and was awarded the Nobel Peace Prize in 1964, but in 1968 he was shot dead by an assassin. By that time the civil rights battle was almost won, but poverty remained an issue – especially the poverty of blacks in the South and in the slum "ghettos" of the northern cities. There was still a long way to go.

*Moved and inspired, Martin Luther King's fellow marchers cheer his speech. Heard by some 200,000 people in Washington, D.C., King's "dream" made a great impact at the time. It was reported in newspapers and seen on film and television and is now regarded as a classic statement of human aspirations.*

## What the papers said

The national conscience … has been stirred…. The only question is whether the translation of attitude into action will come fast enough to prevent new explosions of interracial violence. The unity of Negro and white citizens in the leadership of the march and in its rank and file demonstrated the indivisibility of the fight for genuine equality in all phases of American affairs. It was a rebuke to those in both races … who favor a pulling-apart instead of a pulling-together.

*The New York Times, August 30, 1963*

- **FURTHER INFORMATION**
- 📖 Books:
  *Days that Shook the World: The Dream of Martin Luther King* by Liz Gogerly (Wayland, 2003)
- Websites:
  www.spartacus.schoolnet.co.uk/USAkingML.htm
  The life and achievements of Martin Luther King

# The President Is Assassinated

It happened at about 12:30 P.M., as the motorcade moved slowly through the streets of Dallas, the second largest city in Texas. Behind the first car and police motorcyclists, a dark blue, open-topped Lincoln automobile drove at 11 miles per hour through streets lined with armed police and cheering people. Inside the Lincoln sat Texas Governor John Connally and his wife. The back seat held the guests of honor, President John F. Kennedy and his wife Jackie, newly arrived in the city on the second day of a visit to Texas.

### Kennedy is shot

The couple were waving to the crowd when shots were heard. The president fell forward, crying "My God, I'm hit!" and clutched his throat. Governor Connally, also hit, was covered in blood. Then there was another shot, and Kennedy was flung backward. The bullet had blown a hole in his head, and Jackie Kennedy screamed as blood and brain tissue spattered the car. The president fell into his wife's arms as the Lincoln accelerated. Now leading the motorcade, it raced to the nearby Parkland Memorial Hospital. Despite emergency surgery, the president was pronounced dead at 1 P.M.

*President Kennedy and his wife Jackie smile at the crowds lining the streets of Dallas to greet them. Minutes later, despite the heavy security around the motorcade, shots rang out and an assassin's bullets mortally wounded the president.*

## The likely assassin

Reports suggested that the shots were fired from one of the tall buildings lining the route, a schoolbook warehouse. Among its employees was Lee Harvey Oswald, a young man whose erratic past included a period living in the Soviet Union. Pursued, Oswald took refuge in a movie theater, where he was arrested. He protested his innocence, but on November 24, before the investigation had got very far, he was shot dead while being transferred to the county jail. The killer, a nightclub owner named Jack Ruby, claimed to have acted to avenge Jackie Kennedy.

## A conspiracy?

There was convincing evidence to link Oswald with the rifle and cartridges found on the sixth floor of the warehouse, and in 1964 the specially appointed Warren Commission concluded that he had acted alone. But many contradictory facts remained unaccounted for, and later investigators believed that there might have been more than one gunman acting as part of a conspiracy, rather than a single, presumably unhinged individual. One plausible theory blamed the Mafia, a powerful criminal organization that was under investigation by Kennedy's administration. However, it now seems unlikely that the full story behind Kennedy's death will ever be known.

*November 24, 1963, Dallas police station: Jack Ruby shoots Lee Harvey Oswald, the alleged assassin of President Kennedy.*

# What the papers said

Word of President Kennedy's assassination struck the world's capitals with shattering impact, leaving heads of state and the man in the street stunned and grief-stricken…. Pubs in London and cafes in Paris fell silent, as the news came over radio and television. In Moscow, a Russian girl walked weeping along the street. At UN headquarters in New York, delegates of 11 nations bowed their heads in a moment of silence. In Buenos Aires, newspapers sounded sirens reserved for news of the utmost gravity…. Sir Winston Churchill branded the slaying a monstrous act.

*The Dallas Morning News,* November 23, 1963

- **SEE ALSO**
Pages 12–13: October 22, 1962: The Cuban Missile Crisis

- **FURTHER INFORMATION**
  Books:
  *Days that Shook the World: The Kennedy Assassination* by Liz Gogerly (Wayland, 2002)
  Websites:
  www.archives.gov/research/jfk
  JFK assassination records

# Beatlemania Hits the U.S.

After the plane touched down at Kennedy Airport in New York, fans broke through the police line and thousands fought to see the Beatles. No other British pop group had received such a reception in the United States. Over the next two weeks, the Beatles were pursued and were often in danger of being mobbed at every stage of their visit. Their U.S. triumph confirmed that they were not merely stars in Britain and Europe, but had become a worldwide phenomenon.

### Four young men

The Beatles were four young men from Liverpool, England – John Lennon, Paul McCartney, George Harrison, and Ringo Starr. Most of the group had worked together since the late 1950s, but they had become the Beatles only in 1960. Their distinctive image – brushed-forward hair and neat "mod" suits – was even more recent, dating from shortly before their first recording in 1962, *Love Me Do*. It was moderately successful, but their next single, *Please Please Me*, reached number one in the UK charts, and one hit followed another throughout 1963. Beatlemania swept Britain, and in November, the Beatles appeared at the Royal Variety Performance.

*The Beatles arrive at Kennedy Airport and get an indication of the welcome they will receive everywhere in the United States. Waving and smiling, they are (left to right) John Lennon, Paul McCartney, George Harrison (guitars), and Ringo Starr (drums).*

## A new sound

Liverpool was a major center of rock music in the 1960s, and other successful groups from there included Gerry and the Pacemakers and the Searchers. But the Beatles made an incomparable impression. At this time their songs, many written by the Lennon-McCartney partnership, were in the heavy "Merseybeat" style, but with some individual touches and with distinctive high "oohs" that became a Beatles trademark.

Their group personality was a significant part of the Beatles' impact. They were young, working class and cheekily irreverent without being really offensive. Seemingly ordinary, they appealed to the youth culture that was such a feature of the 1960s. Their success in the USA was the start of a cult of Britishness, when 'swinging London' became the centre of youth fashion, with miniskirts by Mary Quant, and Carnaby Street the place to buy trendy clothes.

## Later years

The Beatles proved to have unusual musical talents. Lennon and McCartney, and later George Harrison, went on to compose many strikingly original songs, notably for the 1967 album *Sgt. Pepper's Lonely Hearts Club Band*. They remained responsive to the popular mood, adopting much of the hippy outlook of the later 1960s. In 1970, the Beatles broke up but remained individually active. John Lennon died in 1980, assassinated outside his New York apartment.

*American teenagers scream with emotion during a performance by the Beatles at the Coliseum, Washington, D.C., in February 1964.*

## What the papers said

About 500 teenagers, most of them girls, had shown up at the Plaza [Hotel].... One group of girls asked everybody who came out, "Did you see the Beatles? Did you touch them?" A policeman came up, and one of them yelled, "He touched a Beatle! I saw him!" The girls jumped on the cop's arms and back, but it wasn't a mob assault. There were goony smiles all over their faces.

Tom Wolfe, *New York Herald Tribune*, February 8, 1964

- **SEE ALSO**
Pages 38–39: August 15, 1969: The First Day at Woodstock
Pages 44–45: January 15, 1967: The First Super Bowl Is Played

- **FURTHER INFORMATION**
Books:
*People Who Made History: The Beatles* edited by David M. Haugen (Greenhaven, 2005)
Websites:
www.beatles.com
The Beatles' official website

# The Marines Arrive in Vietnam

Two battalions of U.S. Marines waded ashore at Da Nang in South Vietnam, where the U.S. air base had to be protected against communist guerrillas. There were only 3,500 Marines, but they were the first contingent of American combat troops to be sent to Vietnam. In June they saw action for the first time and by the end of 1965 another 18,000 troops had landed. The United States had become deeply involved in a Southeast Asian conflict that, despite its military might, it would fail to win.

*Marines come ashore from landing craft at Da Nang. Their arrival marked the beginning of an increasingly costly and demoralizing U.S. involvement in the South Vietnam conflict.*

## Divided country

Vietnam was a French colony until 1954, when it was divided into a communist northern state, led by Ho Chi Minh, and an anti-communist South Vietnam. Determined to prevent the spread of communism, the United States supported the South Vietnamese dictator Ngo Dinh Diem. A communist resistance movement, the Viet Cong, became active in the south during the early 1960s, supplied by North Vietnam down the "Ho Chi Minh trail" – well-concealed jungle paths along the frontiers of neighboring Cambodia and Laos. President Kennedy stepped up the American effort, sending substantial aid and increasing the U.S. presence to 15,000 "advisers" to prop up the South Vietnamese army.

## Deepening conflict

Under Kennedy's successor, Lyndon B. Johnson, the United States became even more deeply involved. In 1964, the United States began a devastating bombing campaign against North Vietnam. The direct involvement of the United States in the war ultimately drew in over half a million Americans. The Viet Cong's jungle hideouts gave them some protection, but U.S. bombs, shells, and napalm took a heavy toll.

Despite U.S. help, South Vietnam's forces performed badly. The United States carried a heavy burden and by the end of the conflict had lost 58,000 men. By 1967, more and more Americans were joining antiwar protests, bitterly dividing and demoralizing the country.

## Withdrawal and defeat

The turning point was the January 1968 Tet Offensive, when the Viet Cong for a time held South Vietnamese cities and penetrated into the heart of the capital, Saigon. President Johnson refused requests to send more troops and, soon afterwards, started peace talks with North Vietnam. The violence was far from over, but U.S. forces withdrew between 1969 and 1973, leaving a supposedly reinvigorated and re-equipped South Vietnamese army to carry on. They failed to stem the tide, and in 1975, the communist forces achieved total victory, ending the Vietnam War.

*Civilians flee from the fighting in Saigon during the Tet Offensive launched by the Viet Cong in May 1968.*

## eye witness

I was walking in a single file of Vietnamese soldiers along the narrow banks that divided the paddy fields of the Mekong delta…. When the shell burst, my impression was that a small volcano had sprung out of the ground…. I felt a tremendous shudder through the soles of my boots, and then the blast threw me to the ground…. My heart thumped and my hands shook. Then I heard a half sob, half gasp…. it was my friend from Nha Trang, clasping his stomach…. He was dying.

Gavin Young, *Slow Boats to China* (Hutchinson, 1981)

- **SEE ALSO**
  Pages 30–31: May 10, 1968: The Barricades Rise in Paris

- **FURTHER INFORMATION**
  - Books:
    *How Did It Happen: The Vietnam War* by Clive Gifford (Franklin Watts, 2005)
  - Websites:
    www.vietnamwar.com
    History of the Vietnam War

# The Cultural Revolution Erupts

After months of political maneuvers, debates, and demonstrations, it was official. On August 8, 1966, the Central Committee of the Chinese Communist Party proclaimed the "16 points" of a program that would guide the Great Proletarian Cultural Revolution.

## Mao Zedong

The driving force behind the Cultural Revolution was the legendary Mao Zedong, under whose leadership the Communist Party had seized power in 1949. Now in his 70s, Mao was revered but had lost political influence during the 1960s. The Cultural Revolution involved, among other things, Mao's return to power and the elimination of hostile factions within the government. But Mao also genuinely believed that China's ruling Communist Party had lost much of its revolutionary fervor and was becoming a privileged elite. Moreover, old pre-communist values were still lingering, so mass action was needed to root out "the four olds" – old ideas, old culture, old customs, old habits.

## ⊙ eye witness

I saw a dozen or so teachers standing on the platform on the sports ground, with their heads bent and their arms twisted [behind them].... some were kicked on the back of their knees and forced to kneel, while others, including my English-language teacher, an elderly man ... were forced to stand on long, narrow benches. He ... swayed and fell, cutting his forehead on the sharp corner of a bench. A Red Guard standing next to him instinctively stooped and extended his hand to help, but immediately straightened up ... yelling: "Get back onto the bench!" He did not want to be seen as soft.

Jung Chang describes a "denunciation meeting" during her schooldays in *Wild Swans* (Flamingo, 1993)

## Red Guards

To achieve his aims, Mao looked for help to the army, led by his ally Lin Piao, and to the millions of Chinese students, organized into militant Red Guards. Flourishing the famous "Little Red Book" of Chairman Mao's thoughts, the Red Guards moved through the country, denouncing and humiliating officials, teachers, writers, and artists. Huge numbers of people were exiled to the countryside to be "reeducated" by hard work.

Red Guards destroyed many "old" works of art, and schools, universities, temples, and churches were closed. In some places, Red Guards set up committees as rivals to the existing authorities.

*Standing in front of a picture of Mao, young Chinese read from their copies of the "Little Red Book" of Mao's sayings, the approved text for aspiring Cultural Revolutionaries.*

Where officials resisted, a situation close to civil war developed. The Red Guards themselves split into factions and fought one another.

## Chaos and disaster

By 1968, the situation in China was so chaotic that Mao called a halt to the Cultural Revolution, without admitting that it had been a disaster. The Cultural Revolution was said to have achieved its aims, which was true only in that Mao had removed all his leading rivals. Mao's chosen successor, army chief Lin Piao, was the next to go, killed in a plane crash in 1971 while fleeing after a failed coup attempt. The Cultural Revolution caused immense suffering and its effects on Chinese society and its economy lasted for many years. Mao remained in charge until his death in 1976, after which new leaders set China on a radically different course.

• **FURTHER INFORMATION**
📖 Books:
*20th Century Perspectives: The Rise of Modern China* by Tony Allan (Heinemann, 2002)
Websites:
www.historylearningsite.co.uk/cultural_revolution.htm
The Cultural Revolution

# Biafra Breaks Away from Nigeria

The Republic of Biafra was born on May 30, 1967. Colonel Odumegwu Ojukwu, military governor of Nigeria's Eastern Region, declared that the region had become the sovereign state of Biafra and no longer owed allegiance to Nigeria. The Nigerian ruler, Colonel Yakubu Gowon, denounced the breakaway and predicted that it would be short-lived.

## Military coups

A large and heavily populated country in West Africa, Nigeria had been a British colony until 1960. It was a land of widely different peoples, and old antagonisms surfaced when Nigeria ran into economic problems. In January 1966, an army coup overthrew its notoriously corrupt civilian government. The new military regime was dominated by officers belonging to the Ibo people, but in July 1966, it was overthrown by a rival army faction, mostly from the northern tribes, which made Colonel Gowon head of state.

## Massacres

Two months later, there was unrest in the north, and savage attacks were made on the Ibos. Their homeland was in the Eastern Region, but large numbers had emigrated to other parts of Nigeria. Like immigrants in many countries, the Ibos were often unpopular, and the attacks on them turned into large-scale massacres. An estimated 30,000 Ibos were killed, and half a million of them fled back to the Eastern Region.

Gowon had done little to stop the massacres, adding to the Ibos' fears. When he published plans for territorial changes unfavorable to the Ibos, Ojukwu proclaimed an independent Biafra. Although relatively small, Biafra did have the advantage of being rich in oil. This was Nigeria's major natural resource, so Gowon's government was quite determined not to accept the breakaway.

*Yakubu Gowon, head of Nigeria's military government at the time of Biafra's attempt to break away and become independent.*

*Learning to use a rifle: a training camp at Owerri for young Biafran soldiers. After initial instruction, the young men went straight to the front to fight with increasing desperation against Nigerian government forces.*

## War

War broke out on July 6, 1967. Unexpectedly, the Biafrans took the initiative and they managed to advance into the neighboring territory. However, the Biafrans were outnumbered, and the Nigerian government forces slowly drove them back. When Port Harcourt fell in May 1968, Biafra lost its access to the sea and the Shell oil refineries. The war was lost, but the Biafrans fought on stubbornly for 18 months, eventually supplied by only a single airstrip. Though heroic, their efforts brought immense suffering to the Ibo people, at least half a million of whom died from starvation.

Finally, after two and a half years of war, Biafra surrendered in January 1970. Nigeria was reunited but, like so many African states, it was to have a deeply troubled future.

## What the papers said

In Enugu there was dancing in the streets and chanting by massed crowds as the Ojukwu regime went through with the full ceremonies for the proclamation of a new state…. The new Biafran flag – red, black and green with a rising sun device – was hoisted to the accompaniment of a 42-gun salute. Crowds, predominantly Ibos, carried the tree branches that symbolized an occasion of national rejoicing, and shouted: "Biafra, Biafra, we hail thee. Nigeria is dead. We are Biafrans now."
*Guardian*, May 31, 1967

- **SEE ALSO**
  Pages 4–5: March 21, 1960:
  Massacre at Sharpeville
  Pages 6–7: June 30, 1960:
  The Congo Gains its Independence

- **FURTHER INFORMATION**
  Books:
  *World in Focus: Nigeria* by Ali Brownlie Bojang
  (Wayland, 2006)
  Websites:
  www.nigeria-planet.com/The-Nigerian-Civil-War.html
  The Nigerian civil war

# Israeli Strikes Launch the Six-Day War

At 8:45 A.M., Egyptian time, Israeli aircraft struck hard at Egypt's airfields. They achieved complete surprise. Wave after wave of planes followed, relentlessly bombing and strafing the Egyptian airfields and then returning to their bases. There, they were refueled, reloaded, and sent back into action so rapidly that Egyptian observers believed the Israelis must be receiving help from other air forces. Most Egyptian planes were destroyed on the ground, but some managed to take off, only to be shot down in dogfights. Within three hours, the main onslaught was over. The Egyptians had lost almost 300 aircraft.

## Israel's victory

In one day of fighting, Israel had established an overwhelming superiority in the air that would give it a decisive advantage in the war that followed. Meanwhile, Israeli ground forces had attacked Egyptian positions in Gaza and the Sinai Peninsula. Israeli hopes of taking on only a single opponent were dashed when Jordan, Syria, and Iraq declared war. However, Israeli forces won decisive victories and occupied Gaza, the Sinai Peninsula, the West

*Triumphant offensive: Israeli armor surges into Egypt during the Six-Day War.*

## ◉ eye witness

There must be at least 10,000 vehicles abandoned in Sinai; some are total wrecks, others untouched…. In the Mitla Pass two miles of vehicles, soft-skinned and armored, nose to tail, had been wrecked and wrecked again by air attack. Other convoys lay like broken-backed snakes across the desert roads. At other times it was like flying over a table exercise [war game], with whole tank squadrons in formation knocked out…. Claims of 500 tanks knocked out must be valid and may be an underestimate.

**Charles Douglas-Home in** *The Times,* **June 11, 1967**

Bank, and East Jerusalem. Finally, they stormed the Golan Heights, an area of southern Syria that had long been used to bombard Israeli settlements on the other side of the frontier.

*Desperate flight: though this bridge has been wrecked, Palestinian refugees from the West Bank make their way across it to reach Jordan during the Six-Day War.*

## An ongoing conflict

In six days, Israel had changed the map of the Middle East. But the problems that had caused the war had not gone away. The conflict began when increasing Jewish settlement in Palestine in the early 20th century aroused Arab antagonism. In 1948, Palestine was partitioned (split) and the Jewish state of Israel was set up. Israel was attacked by the neighboring Arab states, but survived.

Meanwhile, many thousands of Palestinian Arabs fled or were driven from their homes. They became refugees, living in camps in neighboring states or the parts of Palestine held by Arab states – Gaza by Egypt, East Jerusalem and the West Bank by Jordan.

The situation remained unchanged after a second war in 1956. Then in 1967, Israel again seemed threatened by its neighbors and decided to strike first. Israel's victory brought many Palestinians under its rule, a fact that complicated rather than resolved the conflict. The Arab-Israel issue was still troubling the world in the 21st century.

• **FURTHER INFORMATION**

📖 **Books:**
*Timelines: The Arab-Israeli Conflict*
by Cath Senker (Franklin Watts, 2007)

🖰 **Websites:**
news.bbc.co.uk/onthisday/hi/witness/june/5/
newsid_4583000/4583291.stm
Memories of the 1967 Arab-Israeli war

# The First Human Heart Transplant

Louis Washkansky, a 55-year-old South African grocer, suffered from diabetes and an incurable heart condition that was certain to kill him within weeks. His only chance was to undergo an operation that had never yet been performed: the removal of his diseased heart and its replacement by a healthy organ.

## A daunting challenge

The obstacles were formidable. The replacement could only come from a dead person whose heart was still beating. And since the heart deteriorates rapidly after death, the operation would have to be carried out very quickly. A further problem was that the human immune system rejects foreign

*Dr. Christiaan Barnard shows an X-ray image of his patient Louis Washkansky's chest, taken during the first heart transplant operation.*

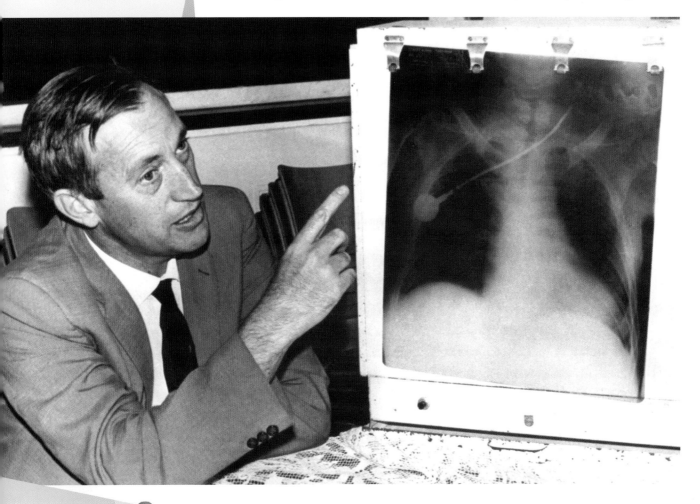

materials. However, the heart of a young woman who had been killed in an automobile accident became available, and the chances of success were increased by the fact that she had the same blood type as Washkansky. The odds were further improved by the use of drugs that weakened the patient's immune system.

## The operation

The operation was carried out by Dr. Christiaan Barnard and a team of 20 surgeons at the Groote Schuur Hospital in Cape Town, South Africa. It lasted for five hours. Most of Washkansky's heart was removed and he was kept alive by a heart-lung machine, which took over the function of the removed organ, oxygenating the blood and pumping it into the main arteries. Then the donor heart was sewn onto the connective tissues. It was smaller than the organ it replaced, which meant that it would have to work harder to do its job. The critical moment came when Barnard applied electrodes to the new heart, shocking it into a regular beat. Washkansky was going to survive.

The operation created a worldwide sensation, but its real success was limited. Because of the drugs that suppressed Washkansky's immune system, he was unable to fight off infections. Eighteen days after the operation, he died of pneumonia. Barnard's second transplant patient, Philip Blaiberg, lived for 19 months, but in general survival rates were poor.

> ## ⊙ **eye** witness
>
> A 20-joule charge of [electricity] … shot through the squirming muscles, causing the body of Louis Washkansky to arch upward as though kicked in the back. For a moment the heart lay paralysed, without any sign of life. We waited – it seemed like hours – until it slowly began to relax. Then it came like a bolt of light. There was a sudden contraction of the atria, followed quickly by the ventricles in obedient response – then the atria, and again the ventricles. Little by little it began to roll with the lovely rhythm of life, the heartbeat of the world.
>
> *Christiaan Barnard recalls the operation in* One Life *(George G. Harrap & Co. Ltd., 1970)*

## Progress

For a time it looked as though heart transplants were more spectacular than useful. But the development of the immunosuppressant cyclosporine and other improvements in treatment transformed patients' chances of living for years rather than months. In 1981, the success of a triple transplant – heart, liver, and lungs – demonstrated the immense advances made by medical science and confirmed Christiaan Barnard's place in medical history.

• **FURTHER INFORMATION**
📖 **Books:**
*Heart Transplants* by Nancy Hoffman (Lucent Books, 2003)
*Organ Transplantation* by Carol Ballard (Franklin Watts, 2007)
🖱 **Websites:**
www.bbc.co.uk/health/donation/factfilesod_history.shtml
A history of organ transplants

# Barricades Rise in Paris

After days of violent clashes between students and police, on May 10, 1968, students prepared to defend the Latin Quarter, site of Paris's ancient university, the Sorbonne. They threw up 60 barricades, made with piled-up paving stones and overturned vehicles. At around 2:15 A.M., riot police attacked with clubs, tear gas, and stun grenades, while the students took shelter behind the barricades and flung paving stones and some home-made gas bombs.

## Strikes and protests

Not for the first time, the police acted with an extreme brutality that united students and local residents against them. There were protests all over France, and on May 13, a one-day general strike took place. Around 800,000 people marched through Paris, calling for an end to General Charles de Gaulle's ten-year rule. Soon the students had occupied the Sorbonne and millions of workers went on strike, taking over their factories and offices. France seemed to be on the verge of revolution.

In reality, there was no plan to take power. People began to tire of endless disruption, and concessions to the workers and students weakened their enthusiasm. On June 16, the 200 students left in the Sorbonne were evicted without trouble by the police. On June 30, de Gaulle's supporters won a landslide victory in a general election.

*May 1968: Parisian students fling stones at the riot police during a period of violent clashes. For a time it seemed as though France was on the brink of revolution.*

## Student movements

France's "student revolt" was not an isolated event. Militancy among young people, especially students, was widespread in the 1960s, starting with black and white U.S. students who took part in the struggle for civil rights. Most student movements began with specific grievances about campus restrictions or teaching. A minority held radical political views, mainly of a "New Left" type – socialist and would-be revolutionary, but opposed to the rigid, oppressive socialism associated with Soviet communism. In France, New Leftists like Daniel Cohn-Bendit, known as "Danny the Red," became increasingly prominent as the student movement became radicalized.

The New Left owed much of its short-lived influence to the Vietnam War. More than any other issue, this turned students to militancy, starting in the United States at Berkeley, California, in 1964. Student unrest spread to the universities and art colleges of Britain, to France, West Germany, and Italy. Everywhere students used similar disruptive tactics – sit-ins (occupation of university buildings) and teach-ins (debates), as well as demonstrations and marches. Student movements went on into the early 1970s before fading away, their more ambitious hopes unfulfilled.

*The evacuation of the Sorbonne by police in June 1968. Some students left of their own accord. Others had to be removed by force.*

• **SEE ALSO**
Pages 14–15: August 28, 1963:
The "I Have a Dream" Speech
Pages 20–21: March 8, 1965:
The Marines Arrive in Vietnam

• **FURTHER INFORMATION**
Websites:
libcom.org/history/1968-the-may-june-uprising-in-france
The French student revolt

# Soviet Forces Invade Czechoslovakia

The invasion began on the night of August 20, 1968. Most Czechoslovaks realized what had happened only when they awoke the next morning and saw Soviet tanks in the streets. The Soviets and their allies claimed that they had been invited in to protect the country, but this was soon shown to be a lie. The main Czech authorities refused to be intimidated and denounced the occupation. And although armed resistance would have been futile against the overwhelming strength of the invaders, ordinary people made their furious feelings clear, the boldest actually climbing onto tanks and arguing with their crews. The Soviets quickly tightened their grip, taking over the government and media and arresting the Czech leader, Alexander Dubcek.

*May 1968, before the storm: Czech leader Alexander Dubcek is greeted with joy by supporters of his reform program. Talks with the Soviet leadership appeared to have succeeded, but three months later, the Soviets invaded.*

## The Prague Spring

The invasion ended an exciting experiment. Czechoslovakia was a communist state and one of the East European allies of the Soviet Union. (Since 1992, Czechoslovakia has been replaced by two states, the Czech and Slovak republics.) The communist states had socialist systems in which the entire economy was run by the state, supposedly for the benefit of the people. But any advantages the system may have had were outweighed by the dominant role played by the Communist Party and the lack of political rights and freedom of speech, which had led to terrible abuses.

Dubcek became the Czech leader in January 1968 and by April, he had launched a full-scale reform program. Censorship was lifted, past crimes were investigated, and basic freedoms began to be established. This was to be "socialism with a human face." Delighted Czechs called it the Prague Spring.

## The Soviet response

Dubcek knew that his program would alarm the Soviet Union and he repeatedly insisted on his loyalty to the Soviet-led military alliance, the Warsaw Pact. Yet he underestimated the Soviet leaders' fear that Czech reforms might inspire calls for change in other communist regimes. After months of fruitless high-level meetings and thinly veiled threats, the Soviets and their Warsaw Pact allies acted.

The strong reaction against the invasion persuaded the Soviets to move cautiously. Dubcek was allowed to stay in office and hoped to carry out at least some reforms. However, the balance of power within the Czech Communist Party gradually shifted, and in April 1969, Dubcek was forced out. Under his successor, Gustav Husak, the Czechoslovakian government returned to the oppressive ways of the previous regime and the idea of reforming communism was shelved indefinitely.

*Unable to resist the might of the invading Warsaw Pact forces, Czechs nevertheless made it clear that they were outraged. In the capital, Prague, this young man is risking his life by climbing onto a Soviet T-54 tank.*

## eye witness

It was almost 9:00 A.M. when about eight Soviet paratroopers and one or two lower officers burst into my office and closed and blocked the windows and connecting doors. It was like an armed robbery ... the main door flew open again and in walked some higher officers of the KGB, including a highly decorated, very short colonel ... [who] told us that he was taking us "under his protection." Indeed, we were protected, sitting around that table – each of us had a tommy gun pointed at the back of his head.

*Alexander Dubcek's memories of the morning he was arrested, recalled in* Hope Dies Last *(Harper Collins, 1993)*

- **SEE ALSO**
  Pages 8–9: August 13, 1961: The Berlin Wall Rises
  Pages 12–13: October 22, 1962: The Cuban Missile Crisis

- **FURTHER INFORMATION**
  Books:
  *How Did It Happen? The Cold War* by Paul Harrison (Franklin Watts, 2005)
  Websites:
  www.coldwar.org
  The Cold War Museum

# The First Men on the Moon

On July 20, 1969, a lunar module carried Neil Armstrong and Edwin "Buzz" Aldrin down from their spacecraft, Apollo 11, to the surface of the Moon. From the module, nicknamed the Eagle, Armstrong sent Mission Control at Houston, Texas, the first-ever message from the surface: "Houston, Tranquillity Base here. The Eagle has landed." After the astronauts had strapped on their backpacks, Armstrong opened a door, came out of it backward, and climbed down a ladder. He turned on the lunar module's TV camera and then became the first man to set foot on the Moon. Back on Earth, 600 million people watched the event on their TV sets and heard Armstrong declare, "That's one small step for a man, one giant leap for mankind."

## Apollo 11

This was the high point of a voyage that began on July 16, when Apollo 11 left Cape Canaveral, Florida, looking small by comparison with the Saturn rocket on which it rode. The fuel and liquid oxygen in the rocket blasted Apollo out of the Earth's atmosphere. As each step of its job was done, part of the rocket fell away, finally leaving just the Apollo 11 spacecraft to complete the journey.

The spacecraft was made up of three parts: the command module, where the astronauts lived; the service module, which contained the engines and other systems; and the lunar module, which would make the Moon landing. As they approached their target, the astronauts maneuvered Apollo into orbit 69 miles (111 kilometers) above the Moon; Michael Collins remained on board while Armstrong and Aldrin made their historic descent in the lunar module.

*A historic moment: Apollo 11 is launched from pad 39A at Kennedy Space Center, Florida, on July 16, 1969. Four days later, Neil Armstrong and Edwin "Buzz" Aldrin became the first men to set foot on the Moon.*

They spent only a short time on the surface, setting up a memorial and carrying out scientific work, before going back to Apollo 11 for the return journey. On July 24, the command module splashed down in the Pacific with the three astronauts on board.

## The space race

This great achievement received much of its impetus from the Cold War rivalry between the United States and the Soviet Union. In April 1961, the world was astonished to learn that a Soviet army officer, Yuri Gagarin, had become the first man in space. President Kennedy responded by declaring that the United States would put a man on the Moon by the end of the decade. After huge efforts and many rehearsals, the goal was achieved. Five more manned Moon landings were made up to 1975, after which the emphasis shifted to unmanned flights, further and further out into space.

*Walking on the surface of the Moon: Buzz Aldrin steps out at Tranquillity Base, in a photograph taken by fellow astronaut Neil Armstrong.*

## eye witness

Of all the spectacular views we had, the most impressive to me was on the way to the Moon, when we flew through its shadow. We were still thousands of miles away, but ... the Moon almost filled our circular window. It was eclipsing the Sun ... and the corona of the Sun was visible around the limb of the Moon as a gigantic lens-shaped or saucer-shaped light, stretching out to several lunar diameters. It was magnificent, but the Moon was even more so ... no part of it illuminated by the Sun. It was illuminated only by earthshine.

Neil Armstrong recalls a magic moment in *First on the Moon: A Voyage with Neil Armstrong, Michael Collins, Edwin E. Aldrin Jr*, written with Gene Farmer and Dora Jane Hamblin (Michael Joseph, 1970)

• **FURTHER INFORMATION**
📖 Books:
*Days That Shook the World: The Moon Landing* by Paul Mason (Wayland, 2002)
🖱 Websites:
www.nasa.gov
NASA's official website

# British Troops Arrive in Northern Ireland

British forces were sent to Northern Ireland as a temporary measure, to restore order. Fierce fighting had broken out in the province between Protestants and Catholics; the police in Belfast had shot many civilians; and in the Bogside area of Londonderry, besieged Catholics had put up barricades. When the troops arrived they were welcomed as protectors, and the barricades were taken down.

*August 1969: the Bogside, a Catholic area of the mainly Protestant city of Londonderry, was virtually besieged by hostile neighbors and police. The "Battle of the Bogside" was a key factor in the decision by the British government to send troops into Northern Ireland.*

## Origin of the conflict

Northern Ireland's problems were rooted in the 300-year period when Britain ruled all of Ireland and hostility between Catholics and Protestants created deeply divided communities. In 1921, most of Ireland became self-governing and eventually transformed itself into an independent, overwhelmingly Catholic republic.

The north, where Protestants were a majority, remained part of the UK. Though subject to the British government, it had its own parliament at Stormont and was mostly left to manage its own affairs. Stormont rule was nakedly unjust. The political system was manipulated to deny any influence to the large Catholic minority (about a third of the population), which was discriminated against in the areas of jobs and housing. The police (RUC) and a volunteer reserve (B Specials) were instruments of this Protestant, or "Loyalist" regime. The only resistance came from the IRA (Irish Republican Army), a militant underground organization that had never accepted the partition of Ireland. However, its campaigns achieved little, and by the 1960s, it was pursuing a political rather than a military strategy.

## The troubles

The situation was transformed in 1968 by the emergence of a civil rights movement, pledged to secure equal rights for all citizens in the province. But civil rights demonstrations and marches were brutally assaulted, with the RUC and the B Specials prominent among the attackers. The British government pressed the Northern Irish authorities to put through reforms, but resistance to any concessions was strong. Meanwhile, the situation began to deteriorate. A vicious attack on a New Year 1969 civil rights march led to mob violence on both sides, culminating in the disturbances that brought in British troops.

The "temporary" army presence was prolonged as "the troubles" continued in earnest. The IRA resumed military activity, the army's good relations with the Catholic community collapsed, and the Ulster Volunteers and other Protestant equivalents to the IRA went into action. Decades of conflict ensued before the emergence of a peace process in the 1990s led to a cessation of the violence and the hope of a final resolution of the dispute.

British soldiers on a Northern Irish street. Welcomed at first, they soon became targets as the IRA and other armed groups stepped up their activities.

## What the papers said

The decision to put British troops on to the riot-torn streets of Ulster is the right one. Vastly regrettable, but regrettably unavoidable. The government of Major James Chichester-Clark in Northern Ireland has had its chance to bring peace to the region. And it has failed. The first task for the troops is to help restore order. An unenviable job. As the men in the middle, their presence will be resented by extremists on both sides.

*The Daily Mirror, August 15, 1969*

- **FURTHER INFORMATION**
- 📖 Books:
  *Troubled World: The Troubles in Northern Ireland* by Ivan Minnis (Heinemann, 2001)
- Websites:
  www.bbc.co.uk/history/recent/troubles
  An exploration of the Northern Ireland conflict

# 15
## AUGUST
# 1969

# The First Day at Woodstock

Its official name was "The Woodstock Music and Art Fair." It was actually a festival of rock and folk music, the kind of event that regularly brought young people together in the 1960s. However, Woodstock was special, both in its size and in the mood it generated. Over 400,000 people – an extraordinary number – congregated on farmland near Bethel in New York. For three days, despite rain, mud, and primitive facilities, they listened to famous performers such as Joan Baez; Janis Joplin; the Grateful Dead; Crosby, Stills & Nash; the Band; and, from Britain, the Who and Joe Cocker.

Woodstock was billed as "three days of peace and music." The emphasis on peace was not an accident, since mass opposition to the war in Vietnam was at its height and reinforced feelings among the young of being at odds with the older generation.

*The huge crowd at Woodstock, almost all of them young people. Many believed that a new era of peace and love was beginning.*

## The hippie movement

In the early 1960s, the young had tended to enjoy the smart lifestyle and possessions made possible by Western affluence. As the decade went on, the mood changed. Some, especially students, became politically committed. But many others were attracted to hippie values, which encouraged the young to "drop out" – to abandon conventional lives and careers in favor of a liberated lifestyle, often involving the use of perception-altering drugs and some form of communal living. Many more became "weekend dropouts," dressing and living hippie-style during their leisure hours. Among this group there was a strong, idealistic belief that "flower-power" and "peace and love" could change the world without sustained struggle or violence.

## A memorable event

Woodstock was one of the supreme expressions of this outlook, strongly felt by those who were there, and experienced through the film and album of the event by huge numbers who were not. The legendary climax of the event came on the unscheduled fourth morning, when guitarist Jimi Hendrix played a two-hour set in front of a remaining audience of 80,000. At moments in his inventive rendering of the U.S. national anthem, *The Star-Spangled Banner*, he produced sounds like explosions and machine-gun fire, clearly intended to evoke U.S. actions in Vietnam. Woodstock is still remembered for the quality of the music performed and the mood it captured, soon to change as more violent confrontations occurred and different values started to take hold.

*Jimi Hendrix playing his legendary two-hour set on August 18, the morning after the official end of the Woodstock festival.*

## What the papers said

The dreams of marijuana and rock music that drew 300,000 fans and hippies ... had little more sanity than the impulses that drive the lemmings to march to their deaths in the sea. They ended in a nightmare of mud and stagnation that paralyzed Sullivan County for a whole weekend. Surely parents, the teachers and indeed all the adults who helped to create the society which these young people are so feverishly rebelling [against] must bear some responsibility for this outrageous episode.

*The New York Times*, August 16, 1969

- **SEE ALSO**
  Pages 18–19: February 8, 1964: Beatlemania Hits the U.S.
  Pages 20–21: March 8, 1965: The Marines Arrive in Vietnam
  Pages 30–31: May 10, 1968: Barricades Rise in Paris

- **FURTHER INFORMATION**
  Books:
  *20th Century Music: 1960s: Age of Rock* by Malcolm Hayes (Heinemann, 2001)
  Websites:
  www.woodstock69.com
  1969 Woodstock Festival and Concert

# *The Feminine Mystique* is published

In the early 1960s, the world was a different place for women. Society expected them to be wives and mothers. If middle-class women did have jobs, they were likely to be teachers or secretaries and they were paid far less than men. The situation began to change with the publication of *The Feminine Mystique* on February 19, 1963. It is rare for a book to change the world, but *The Feminine Mystique* did just that.

## Betty Friedan

Betty Friedan was a wife, mother, and writer who had graduated from Smith College – an all-woman's school – in 1942. For her 15th reunion in 1957, she sent questionnaires to members of her class and discovered that many were unhappy with their lives as wives and mothers. Friedan surveyed other women and found that many felt the same way. She began to write articles about her findings.

*Betty Friedan, pictured here in 1981, was a pioneer of the women's movement and author of the groundbreaking* The Feminine Mystique.

Friedan developed her ideas into *The Feminine Mystique*. In the book, she discussed the changes that had occurred in the United States. During World War II, with men away fighting, many women entered the workforce and held important jobs. But when the war ended, women were forced out of employment and back into their homes. Many educated, middle-class women felt unfulfilled. As Friedan pointed out, they wanted and needed more.

## The women's movement

*The Feminine Mystique* made many women realize that they could work together to achieve equality. The women's movement became organized. Friedan helped found the National Organization for Women to fight for women's rights. This and other groups demanded such things as equal opportunities and pay, financial independence, and free day care.

When Friedan died in 2006, her obituary in *The New York Times* said that *The Feminine Mystique* "ignited the contemporary women's movement." Women achieved many of their goals, though not all. The effort to pass an Equal Rights Amendment to the Constitution failed in 1982, and while millions of women have entered the workforce at all levels, women today still earn less than men.

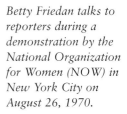

*Betty Friedan talks to reporters during a demonstration by the National Organization for Women (NOW) in New York City on August 26, 1970.*

## ⊙ **eye** witness

The problem that has no name stirring in the minds of so many American women today is not a matter of loss of femininity or too much education, or the demands of domesticity. It is far more important than anyone recognizes.... It may well be the key to our future as a nation and a culture. We can no longer ignore that voice within women that says: "I want something more than my husband and my children and my home."
**Betty Friedan, The Feminine Mystique (1963)**

- **FURTHER INFORMATION**
- 📖 Books:
  *Women of the 1960s* by Stuart Kallen (Lucent Books, 2003)
  *The Women's Rights Movement: Moving Toward Equality* by Shane Mountjoy (Chelsea House, 2007)
- Websites:
  frank.mtsu.edu/~kmiddlet/history/women/wh-timeline.html
  American Women Through Time, with timelines of important events in women's history

# 20
## AUGUST
# 1964

# The War on Poverty Begins

Lyndon B. Johnson became president of the United States under difficult circumstances, taking office when John F. Kennedy was assassinated in November 1963. Within months, however, Johnson made his mark on the presidency by launching the War on Poverty, to make life better for millions of Americans. He signed the landmark legislation enacting the program on August 20, 1964.

### Launching the war

Poverty was a serious problem in 1963, with 35 million Americans living below the poverty line. On January 8, 1964, in his first State of the Union address, Johnson said, "This administration ... declares unconditional war on poverty in America." The War on Poverty was part of a broad vision Johnson had for the country, called the Great Society. Johnson believed that the Great Society would address and solve major problems in healthcare, education, jobs, and the rights of minorities.

Congress quickly passed the Economic Opportunity Act, which Johnson signed on August 20, establishing the Office of Economic Opportunity (OEO). The OEO administered many of the antipoverty programs, which were grouped in three areas. The first was education. Among the education programs created were Head Start, which concentrated on disadvantaged preschool children.

*President Johnson meets with young people at a Philadelphia job opportunity center. As part of his War on Poverty, Johnson created job training programs in partnership with industry.*

42

The creation of jobs was the second area under the OEO. Programs included Job Corps, to supply education, skills training, and work experience for young people. The third area was maintaining income. The Social Security system was changed and benefits were increased, and the minimum wage was raised. Johnson also succeeded in having Congress pass other important measures in 1964 and 1965, including the Civil Rights Act and the Voting Rights Act, to help members of minority groups.

*President Lyndon B. Johnson signs the War on Poverty bill during a ceremony in the White House Rose Garden in Washington, D.C.*

## Success or Failure?

By 1967, popular support for the Great Society programs was declining. Critics assailed the War on Poverty programs for being too big and difficult to coordinate. In later years, most of the programs were dismantled, though some, like Head Start, still exist. Although some critics say the programs encouraged people to become dependent on the government instead of taking personal responsibility for their lives, the programs did help many Americans get a better education and better jobs, as well as access to healthcare and improved housing. The War on Poverty did not end poverty, but by 1968, the poverty rate had fallen to 12.1 percent – roughly the rate it is today.

## eye witness

The use of the term "War on Poverty" was more than a catchy metaphor; it conveyed the hope that it was possible, once and for all, to eliminate poverty from America's cities and streets. The rhetoric of war also suggested the sense of urgency necessary to defeat a well-entrenched enemy, and the level of resources the Johnson administration was willing to commit to the battle

....

**Psychologist Edward Zigler, who helped establish the Head Start program**

- **FURTHER INFORMATION**
  - 📖 Books:
    *The Great Society: America Fights the War on Poverty* by Craig E. Bloom (Lucent Books, 2004)
  - 🖥 Websites:
    www.lbjlib.utexas.edu/johnson/lbjforkids/poverty.shtm
    The War on Poverty site at LBJ for Kids

# The First Super Bowl Is Played

On January 15, 1967, football fans across the country gathered in anticipation. Businesses closed early, and bars were crowded as patrons gathered around the television screens. Everyone was waiting for the live broadcast of the first NFL-AFL World Championship Game. The game had come about as a result of a merger between the National Football League (NFL) and the American Football League (AFL). No one had any idea how popular the game – the Super Bowl – would grow to be, and that "Super Bowl Sunday" would become an unofficial national holiday.

*Green Bay Packers quarterback Bart Starr drops back to pass during the first Super Bowl on January 15, 1967. Starr was named the MVP.*

## A pivotal merger

In 1966, the NFL and AFL agreed to combine, with their respective winners meeting in a championship game. Lamar Hunt, the founder of the AFL – thinking of college bowl games and the toy Super Ball his children played with – suggested calling it the "Super Bowl" as a stopgap measure. The name caught on with both fans and the media, although it did not become official until 1969.

The 1966 season ended with the Green Bay Packers as the NFL champions and the Kansas City Chiefs atop the AFL standings. The Packers, coached by Vince Lombardi, were favored to win the Super Bowl, largely because the AFL was considered inferior. But the Chiefs put up a surprisingly strong fight and trailed by only four points at halftime. At that point, though, the Packers took command and won the game 35–10. "The Chiefs are a mighty good football team," wrote Arthur Dailey in the *New York Times*. "They just happened to meet a better one."

In 1970, the two leagues were officially merged into a combined league with two conferences. The winners of the two conferences now meet in the Super Bowl on the first Sunday in February. The winning team receives the Vince Lombardi Trophy, named after the Packers coach.

## Making history

But it was the first Super Bowl that made history. That game was the only Super Bowl to be telecast by two U.S. networks, CBS and NBC. The game was attended by 61,946 people in the Los Angeles Memorial Coliseum. Fans complained about the top ticket price of $12. (By Super Bowl XLIII, to be played in February 2009, the top ticket price was set at $1000.) Meanwhile, an estimated 60 million watched on TV.

Today, the Super Bowl is the most watched television show of the year – 97.5 million people watched Super Bowl XLII in February 2008 – and the second largest food consumption day of the year, behind Thanksgiving.

The Super Bowl has become a showcase for elaborate and expensive TV commercials. One-minute ads during the first Super Bowl cost between $75,000 and $85,000. During Super Bowl XLII, some marketers were paying as much as $3 million for a 30-second spot. Some viewers watch the game mainly to see the commercials. Others tune in for the halftime show, which has become increasingly elaborate over the years.

*Green Bay Packers coach Vince Lombardi celebrates his team's victory in the first Super Bowl.*

## ⊙ eye witness

New York was gripped by a giddy fever yesterday that began rising at 4 P.M., reached a peak at dusk and began dropping at nightfall. Before the fever finally broke, a vague madness swept the city: little boys refused to go to the movies, big boys refused to speak, girls – little and big – stormed into the kitchens, slammed the door and waited ... "It's impossible," cried Mrs. Lucretia Amari of Brooklyn, while her husband ... stared at the Super Bowl football game on television. "He's obsessed with watching all those big lugs on the idiot box ..."

*New York Times*, January 16, 1967

● FURTHER INFORMATION

📖 Books:
The Making of the Super Bowl: The Inside Story of the World's Greatest Sporting Event by Don Weiss with Chuck Day (McGraw-Hill, 2002)

🖰 Websites:
www.nfl.com/superbowl/history
Super Bowl History, from the official website of the National Football League

# People of the Decade

**Moshe Dayan**
*(1915–1981)*
Born in British-ruled Palestine, Dayan joined the underground Jewish army. He fought in World War II, adopting his distinctive black patch after losing an eye. After Israel's establishment in 1948, he quickly rose through the ranks. As chief of staff he planned the 1956 Israeli campaign against Egypt. In 1967, he was appointed minister of defense and became chief architect of Israel's victory in the Six-Day War. Later in his political career, however, he advocated giving back most of the conquered territories.

**Betty Friedan**
*(1921–2006)*
U.S. writer Betty Friedan was convinced that many women were (like herself) dissatisfied with their lives. In *The Feminine Mystique* (1963), she argued that society forced them into dependency on men and limited roles as wives, mothers, and homemakers. Highly controversial at the time, the book is now recognized as a pioneering feminist text. Friedan was also an active campaigner, co-founding and leading influential bodies such as the National Organization for Women (NOW).

**Ernesto "Che" Guevara**
*(1928–1963)*
Angered by mass poverty, Argentine-born Guevara supported radical causes in Guatemala and then in Cuba, where he fought alongside Fidel Castro against the Fulgencio Batista dictatorship. After Castro's 1959 victory, Guevara held government posts until his departure from Cuba in 1965. He hoped to start new revolutions, first in the Congo and then in Bolivia. In Bolivia, however, he was wounded, captured, and shot. Posters made his image world-famous and turned him into a legend.

**Lyndon Baines Johnson**
*(1908–1973)*
A Texan, Johnson became a senator and a leading member of the Democratic Party. From 1961 he was John F Kennedy's vice-president, taking over as president when Kennedy was assassinated in November 1963. As the champion of the 1964 Civil Rights Act and other reforms, Johnson visualized the United States as "the Great Society." He won the 1964 presidential election, but his second term was mired in controversy over his commitment to the Vietnam War.

**John F. Kennedy**
*(1917–1963)*
In 1960, U.S. politician John F. Kennedy became the nation's first Roman Catholic president. At a time when politicians were mostly elderly, he was relatively young, as well as wealthy and good looking; he and his wife Jackie were seen as uniquely glamorous. Kennedy pursued liberal policies and ably handled the 1962 Cuban Missile Crisis. His assassination shocked the world. His brother Robert (1925–1968) was also assassinated in the middle of his political career.

**Martin Luther King**
*(1929–1968)*
Baptist minister Martin Luther King was the leader of the civil rights movement to secure equality for African Americans. Originally based in Montgomery, Alabama, he led demonstrations, boycotts, and marches in the South, using nonviolent resistance to unjust laws. The 1964 Civil Rights Act and 1965 Voting Rights Act were largely the result of his efforts. In 1964, King was awarded the Nobel Peace Prize, but four years later he was shot by an assassin.

**Nikita Sergeyevich Khrushchev**
*(1894–1971)*
Soviet politician Nikita Khrushchev effectively became sole leader of his country in 1955. He ended the reign of terror associated with the dictatorship of Joseph Stalin (died 1953), but opposition to Communist Party rule continued to be forbidden. Though pugnacious and erratic, Khrushchev pulled back from the brink of war during the 1962 Cuban Missile Crisis and improved relations with the United States. He lost power in 1964 and was forced to retire.

**Mao Zedong**
*(1893–1976)*
One of the founders of the Chinese Communist Party (1921), Mao became its unchallenged leader when the communist forces were threatened with annihilation, and he led them on a famous 6,000-mile (9,650-kilometer) "Long March" to safety (1934–1936). After the communist victory in 1949, Mao became head of the new Chinese People's Republic. He carried through major changes such as China's break with the Soviet Union and the Cultural Revolution, remaining in power until his death.

# Glossary

**abortion** A procedure to end a pregnancy by removing the embryo or fetus from the womb.

**apartheid** The political system that operated in South Africa between 1948 and 1994. It separated the different peoples living there and gave special privileges to those of European origin.

**atria** Chambers in the heart that pump blood into the ventricles (*see* ventricles).

**bloc** A group of states, usually with similar political or economic values, that stand together.

**blockade** An organized action to seal off a state or territory, preventing people or goods from entering or leaving it.

**B Specials** The Ulster Special Constabulary – the reserve police force of Northern Ireland, abolished in 1970.

**Cold War** The state of nonviolent conflict between the Soviet Union and the United States and their respective allies between 1945 and 1990.

**colony** A territory ruled by another state. Until the 1960s, many parts of Africa were colonies of European states.

**communism** A system in which the state controls wealth and property. In practice, the Soviet Union and other communist states were run exclusively by their Communist Parties.

**coup** A sudden seizure of power.

**decolonization** The process by which states gave up their colonies, some more willingly than others.

**democracy** A system of government in which the leaders have been elected freely and equally by all the citizens of a country.

**diabetes** A group of diseases most commonly caused by excessive blood sugar.

**dictatorship** A political system in which a country is ruled by a person or a small group, without the consent of the people.

**dogfights** Combats between fighter aircraft.

**elite** A group or class that is especially gifted or privileged.

**factions** Groups inside a party or government that have opposing ideas or ambitions.

**feminism** The movement that seeks rights and opportunities for women that are equal to those of men.

**food stamps** Coupons given by the government to needy people that can be used to buy food.

**ghetto** A term that originally described the area in many European cities where Jews were forced to live. It is now often used to describe slum areas in cities anywhere that are crowded with poor and disadvantaged groups.

**guerrillas** Fighters who wage hit-and-run warfare, usually against a stronger enemy. They often take advantage of a mountainous or jungle environment in which they can hide.

**hippie** A person who rejects conventional values and goals and believes in unversal peace and love.

**IRA** Irish Republican Army; until recently, the IRA was an armed group that aimed to overthrow the Northern Irish state and unite the region with the Irish Republic.

**KGB** The secret police of the former Soviet Union.

**Mafia** A powerful criminal organization that originated in Italy and is very active in the United States.

**militancy** Actively, possibly aggressively, working for the triumph of ideas or beliefs.

**napalm** A chemical, including petroleum, which is highly inflammable. Napalm was much used, in flame throwers and bombs, by U.S. forces in Vietnam.

**poverty line** A level of income, based on the price of basic necessities, below which somebody is considered to be living in poverty; usually determined by the government.

**proletarian** A communist term for a worker.

**radical** A person or policy favoring fundamental and far-reaching change.

**RUC** Royal Ulster Constabulary – the Northern Ireland police force (1922–2001).

**segregation** A situation in which different ethnic groups must use different public facilities (for example, schools, transportation, park benches, toilets, and cafés).

**socialism** A political system in which the main industries of a country are owned and run by the state for the general benefit.

**Soviet Union** Also known as the USSR (Union of Soviet Socialist Republics), a country consisting of Russia and a number of other East European, Baltic, and Central Asian countries. The leading communist power, the Soviet Union existed from 1922 to 1991.

**State of the Union address** A message delivered by the president of the United States to Congress each year describing the state of the nation.

**Stormont** The parliament of Northern Ireland.

**strafing** Machine-gunning from a plane of installations or people on the ground.

**ventricles** Chambers in the heart that receive blood from the atria (*see* atria).

# Index
Page numbers in **bold** refer to illustrations